Forty Days of

CELEBRATION

Written and Edited by Elizabeth T. Baxter

A Scripture Journal

COMMON
ENGLISH
BIBLE

Nashville

FORTY DAYS OF CELEBRATION:
A SCRIPTURE JOURNAL

INTRODUCTION

Celebration is one of the hallmarks of the people of God. From the creation of the world, to the exodus of the Hebrew slaves from Egypt, to the return to Jerusalem from the Babylonian captivity, to the birth of Jesus, to the good news in Jesus' teachings, to the resurrection of Jesus, to the gift of the Holy Spirit—God's people have been a people of praise and celebration in response to the mighty acts of God.

Especially during the season of Advent, we are drawn to prepare our hearts for the celebration of the birth of Christ and the continuation of the gospel story. During Advent many churches use the three-year cycle of scripture texts from the Revised Common Lectionary. In addition, churches often make use of an Advent wreath, lighting one candle each Sunday of Advent to celebrate the themes of hope, peace, joy, and love.

In keeping with those traditions, this book will use the lectionary texts for Advent (using readings from years A, B, and C) as the basis for our reflections on celebration. Each of the forty days begins with one or more Advent lectionary texts and includes other scriptures that call us to consider more fully the theme of the day. There are ten meditations under each of the headings of "Hope," "Peace," "Joy," and "Love." The last meditation in each category will use scriptures from the lectionary texts for Christmas Eve or

Christmas Day. The Psalms are often called the prayer book of the Bible, and in the hope that these meditations will lead to prayer, many of the meditations end with a reading from the Psalter or a hymn of praise from scripture.

The lectionary readings for Advent invite us to look back to the promises of God proclaimed by the prophets, to celebrate today in promises fulfilled, and to look forward to celebration as we anticipate the fulfillment of promises longed for yet not fully realized. In these scriptures we find hope—hope for peace, trust, restoration, justice, growth of love, healing, mercy, and the final realization of God's kingdom on earth. In these scriptures we find peace—evidence of peace in confession and repentance, the peace that comes with unity in community, peace that comes from wisdom and good leadership, the peace that accompanies patience, and the longed-for peace in the new creation. In these scriptures we find joy—joy in justice, endurance, trust in God, liberty, community, witness, prayer, obedience, loss of fear, surprise, and the power of God. And finally, in these scriptures we find love—love initiated by God that often manifests in surprising ways, steadfast love that reaches to all people and creatures on earth, love that empowers us to do the seemingly impossible, and love that allows us to live into an unknown future with trust and assurance.

In these readings may the God of hope, peace, joy, and love be revealed to you, and may you be a witness to the world of the hope, peace, joy, and love found in Jesus Christ. This, indeed, is a reason for celebration!

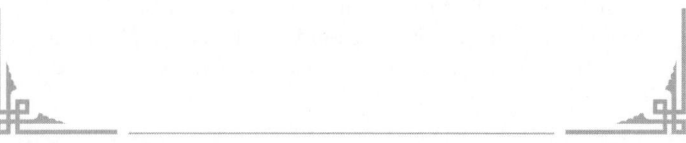

HOPE

DAY 1

Isaiah 2:1-5

This is what Isaiah, Amoz's son, saw concerning Judah and Jerusalem.

In the days to come the mountain of the LORD's house
will be the highest of the mountains.
It will be lifted above the hills;
  peoples will stream to it.
Many nations will go and say,
"Come, let's go up to the LORD's mountain,
  to the house of Jacob's God
    so that he may teach us his ways
    and we may walk in God's paths."
Instruction will come from Zion;
  the LORD's word from Jerusalem.
God will judge between the nations,
  and settle disputes of mighty nations.

Then they will beat their swords into iron plows
 and their spears into pruning tools.
Nation will not take up sword against nation;
 they will no longer learn how to make war.

Come, house of Jacob,
 let's walk by the LORD's light.

Micah 4:1-4

But in the days to come,
 the mountain of the LORD's house
 will be the highest of the mountains;
 it will be lifted above the hills;
 peoples will stream to it.
Many nations will go and say:
 "Come, let's go up to the mountain of the LORD,
 to the house of Jacob's God,
 so that he may teach us his ways
 and we may walk in God's paths!"
Instruction will come from Zion
 and the LORD's word from Jerusalem.
God will judge between the nations
 and settle disputes of mighty nations,
 which are far away.
They will beat their swords into iron plows
 and their spears into pruning tools.
Nation will not take up sword against nation;
 they will no longer learn how to make war.
All will sit underneath their own grapevines,
 under their own fig trees.

There will be no one to terrify them;
for the mouth of the LORD of heavenly forces
has spoken.

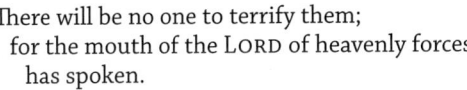

MEDITATION

*The prophets look forward to a day when
all nations will live with peace and justice.
Reflect on actions and attitudes that make
for peace. Where is peace needed in the
world today? Write your own prayer for peace.*

DAY 2

Matthew 24:36-44

"But nobody knows when that day or hour will come, not the heavenly angels and not the Son. Only the Father knows. As it was in the time of Noah, so it will be at the coming of the Human One. In those days before the flood, people were eating and drinking, marrying and giving in marriage, until the day Noah entered the ark. They didn't know what was happening until the flood came and swept them all away. The coming of the Human One will be like that. At that time there will be two men in the field. One will be taken and the other left. Two women will be grinding at the mill. One will be taken and the other left. Therefore, stay alert! You don't know what day the Lord is coming. But you understand that if the head of the house knew at what time the thief would come, he would keep alert and wouldn't allow the thief to break into his house. Therefore, you also should be prepared, because the Human One will come at a time you don't know."

Mark 13:24-27

"In those days, after the suffering of that time, the sun will become dark, and the moon won't give its light. The stars will fall from the sky, and the planets and other heavenly bodies will be shaken. Then they will see the Human One coming in the clouds with great power and splendor. Then he will send the angels and gather together his chosen people from the four corners of the earth, from the end of the earth to the end of heaven."

Psalm 40:1-4

I put all my hope in the LORD.
  He leaned down to me;
  he listened to my cry for help.
He lifted me out of the pit of death,
  out of the mud and filth,
  and set my feet on solid rock.
    He steadied my legs.
He put a new song in my mouth,
  a song of praise for our God.
Many people will learn of this and be amazed;
  they will trust the LORD.
Those who put their trust in the LORD,
  who pay no attention to the proud
  or to those who follow lies,
  are truly happy!

MEDITATION

*The Gospels remind us that we live between
the time of the birth of Jesus and the
anticipated next coming of Christ,
and we are urged to live between the times
in readiness and trust. How do you live
into God's future with trust? What keeps
you from trusting God more completely?*

Day 3

Isaiah 64:1-6

If only you would tear open the heavens
  and come down!
Mountains would quake before you
like fire igniting brushwood or making water boil.
If you would make your name known to your enemies,
the nations would tremble in your presence.

When you accomplished wonders
  beyond all our expectations;
  when you came down, mountains quaked before you.
From ancient times,
  no one has heard,
  no ear has perceived,
  no eye has seen any god but you
  who acts on behalf of those who wait for him!
You look after those who gladly do right;
  they will praise you for your ways.
But you were angry when we sinned;
  you hid yourself when we did wrong.
We have all become like the unclean;
  all our righteous deeds are like a menstrual rag.
All of us wither like a leaf;
  our sins, like the wind, carry us away.

Psalm 13

How long will you forget me, LORD? Forever?
  How long will you hide your face from me?
How long will I be left to my own wits,
  agony filling my heart? Daily?
How long will my enemy keep defeating me?
Look at me!
  Answer me, LORD my God!
Restore sight to my eyes!
  Otherwise, I'll sleep the sleep of death,
    and my enemy will say, "I won!"
    My foes will rejoice over my downfall.

But I have trusted in your faithful love.
  My heart will rejoice in your salvation.
Yes, I will sing to the LORD
  because he has been good to me.

Psalm 30:1-3

I exalt you, LORD, because you pulled me up;
  you didn't let my enemies celebrate over me.
LORD, my God, I cried out to you for help,
  and you healed me.
LORD, you brought me up from the grave,
  brought me back to life from among those
    going down to the pit.

MEDITATION

*Isaiah and the psalmist cry out to God,
believing in God's promises and power in
life's times of trial. How do we, individually
and collectively, hold on to God's promises of
restoration during times of darkness?*

DAY 4

Psalm 80:1-3

Shepherd of Israel, listen!
  You, the one who leads Joseph as if he were a sheep.
  You, who are enthroned
    upon the winged heavenly creatures.
Show yourself before Ephraim,
  Benjamin, and Manasseh!
  Wake up your power!
  Come to save us!
Restore us, God!
  Make your face shine so that we can be saved!

Isaiah 42:1-4a

But here is my servant, the one I uphold;
  my chosen, who brings me delight.
I've put my spirit upon him;
  he will bring justice to the nations.
He won't cry out or shout aloud
  or make his voice heard in public.
He won't break a bruised reed;
  he won't extinguish a faint wick,

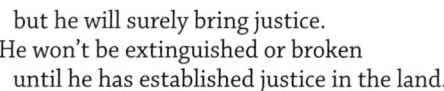

but he will surely bring justice.
He won't be extinguished or broken
until he has established justice in the land.

Amos 5:21-24

I hate, I reject your festivals;
I don't enjoy your joyous assemblies.
If you bring me your entirely burned offerings
and gifts of food—
I won't be pleased;
I won't even look at your offerings
of well-fed animals.
Take away the noise of your songs;
I won't listen to the melody of your harps.
But let justice roll down like waters,
and righteousness like an ever-flowing stream.

Micah 6:8

He has told you, human one, what is good and
what the LORD requires from you:
to do justice, embrace faithful love,
and walk humbly with your God.

MEDITATION

*The prophets declare that God demands that
God's people love justice and act for justice,
and like the psalmist, we often cry out to God
for justice when we experience or witness
injustice. When you pray for justice,
what do you ask of God? How do you work
to make God's justice a reality in the world?*

DAY 5

Romans 13:8-14

Don't be in debt to anyone, except for the obligation to love each other. Whoever loves another person has fulfilled the Law. The commandments, *Don't commit adultery, don't murder, don't steal, don't desire what others have*, and any other commandments, are all summed up in one word: *You must love your neighbor as yourself*. Love doesn't do anything wrong to a neighbor; therefore, love is what fulfills the Law.

As you do all this, you know what time it is. The hour has already come for you to wake up from your sleep. Now our salvation is nearer than when we first had faith. The night is almost over, and the day is near. So let's get rid of the actions that belong to the darkness and put on the weapons of light. Let's behave appropriately as people who live in the day, not in partying and getting drunk, not in sleeping around and obscene behavior, not in fighting and obsession. Instead, dress yourself with the Lord Jesus Christ, and don't plan to indulge your selfish desires.

1 Thessalonians 3:9-13

How can we thank God enough for you, given all the joy we have because of you before our God? Night and day, we pray more than ever to see all of you in person and to complete whatever you still need for your faith. Now may our God and Father himself guide us on our way back to you. May the Lord cause you to increase and enrich your love for each other and for everyone in the same way as we also love you. May the love cause your hearts to be strengthened, to be blameless in holiness before our God and Father when our Lord Jesus comes with all his people. Amen.

Leviticus 19:18

You must not take revenge nor hold a grudge against any of your people; instead, you must love your neighbor as yourself; I am the LORD.

Mark 12:28-34

One of the legal experts heard their dispute and saw how well Jesus answered them. He came over and asked him, "Which commandment is the most important of all?"

Jesus replied, "The most important one is *Israel, listen! Our God is the one Lord, and you must love the Lord your God with all your heart, with all your being, with all your mind, and with all your strength.* The second is this, *You will love your neighbor as yourself.* No other commandment is greater than these."

The legal expert said to him, "Well said, Teacher. You have truthfully said that God is one and there is no other besides him. And to love God with all of the heart, a full understanding, and all of one's strength, and to love one's neighbor as oneself is much more important than all kinds of entirely burned offerings and sacrifices."

When Jesus saw that he had answered with wisdom, he said to him, "You aren't far from God's kingdom." After that, no one dared to ask him any more questions.

MEDITATION

Paul anticipates a day when God's love will be fully realized. As we anticipate that day, we learn to live in love as God loves us. How are you growing in love of God and neighbor? What hinders the growth of love?

DAY 6

1 Corinthians 1:3-9

Grace to you and peace from God our Father and the Lord Jesus Christ.

I thank my God always for you, because of God's grace that was given to you in Christ Jesus. That is, you were made rich through him in everything: in all your communication and every kind of knowledge, in the same way that the testimony about Christ was confirmed with you. The result is that you aren't missing any spiritual gift while you wait for our Lord Jesus Christ to be revealed. He will also confirm your testimony about Christ until the end so that you will be blameless on the day of our Lord Jesus Christ. God is faithful, and you were called by him to partnership with his Son, Jesus Christ our Lord.

Psalm 103:1-14

Let my whole being bless the LORD!
  Let everything inside me bless his holy name!
Let my whole being bless the LORD
  and never forget all his good deeds:
  how God forgives all your sins,

heals all your sickness,
saves your life from the pit,
crowns you with faithful love and compassion,
and satisfies you with plenty of good things
   so that your youth is made fresh like an eagle's.

The LORD works righteousness;
  does justice for all who are oppressed.
God made his ways known to Moses;
  made his deeds known to the Israelites.
The LORD is compassionate and merciful,
  very patient, and full of faithful love.
God won't always play the judge;
  he won't be angry forever.
He doesn't deal with us according to our sin
  or repay us according to our wrongdoing,
  because as high as heaven is above the earth,
  that's how large God's faithful love is for those
   who honor him.
As far as east is from west—
  that's how far God has removed our sin from us.
Like a parent feels compassion for their children—
  that's how the LORD feels compassion
   for those who honor him.
Because God knows how we're made,
  God remembers we're just dust.

MEDITATION

*In faithful love, God bestows grace
on God's people, giving them spiritual gifts
for living faithful lives, and our response
is grateful praise. Where do you see the fruit
of God's spiritual gifts in yourself? In others?
In the body of the church?*

Day 7

Psalm 25:4-7

Make your ways known to me, LORD;
　teach me your paths.
Lead me in your truth—teach it to me—
　because you are the God who saves me.
　　I put my hope in you all day long.
LORD, remember your compassion and faithful love—
　they are forever!
But don't remember the sins of my youth
　or my wrongdoing.
　Remember me only according to your faithful love
　　for the sake of your goodness, LORD.

Ephesians 2:1-7

At one time you were like a dead person because of the things you did wrong and your offenses against God. You used to live like people of this world. You followed the rule of a destructive spiritual power. This is the spirit of disobedience to God's will that is now at work in persons whose lives are characterized by disobedience. At one time you were like those persons. All of you used to do whatever felt good and whatever you thought you wanted so that you were children headed for punishment just like everyone else.

However, God is rich in mercy. He brought us to life with Christ while we were dead as a result of those things that we did wrong. He did this because of the great love that he has for us. You are saved by God's grace! And God raised us up and seated us in the heavens with Christ Jesus. God did this to show future generations the greatness of his grace by the goodness that God has shown us in Christ Jesus.

Luke 6:32-36

"If you love those who love you, why should you be commended? Even sinners love those who love them. If you do good to those who do good to you, why should you be commended? Even sinners do that. If you lend to those from whom you expect repayment, why should you be commended? Even sinners lend to sinners expecting to be paid back in full. Instead, love your enemies, do good, and lend expecting nothing in return. If you do, you will have a great reward. You will be acting the way children of the Most High act, for he is kind to ungrateful and wicked people. Be compassionate just as your Father is compassionate."

MEDITATION

The psalmist pleads for and affirms the mercy of God, and Jesus invites his disciples to reflect the mercy of God in actions with others. When have you shown mercy to another? When have you failed to show mercy? In what things are we tempted to place our trust rather than the mercy of God?

Day 8

Luke 21:25-36

"There will be signs in the sun, moon, and stars. On the earth, there will be dismay among nations in their confusion over the roaring of the sea and surging waves. The planets and other heavenly bodies will be shaken, causing people to faint from fear and foreboding of what is coming upon the world. Then they will see the Human One coming on a cloud with power and great splendor. Now when these things begin to happen, stand up straight and raise your heads, because your redemption is near."

Jesus told them a parable: "Look at the fig tree and all the trees. When they sprout leaves, you can see for yourselves and know that summer is near. In the same way, when you see these things happening, you know that God's kingdom is near. I assure you that this generation won't pass away until everything has happened. Heaven and earth will pass away, but my words will certainly not pass away.

"Take care that your hearts aren't dulled by drinking parties, drunkenness, and the anxieties of day-to-day life. Don't let that day fall upon you unexpectedly, like a trap. It will come upon everyone who lives on the face of the whole earth. Stay alert at all times, praying that you are strong enough to escape everything that is about to happen and to stand before the Human One."

Jeremiah 33:14-16

The time is coming, declares the LORD, when I will fulfill my gracious promise with the people of Israel and Judah. In those days and at that time, I will raise up a righteous branch from David's line, who will do what is just and right in the land. In those days, Judah will be saved and Jerusalem will live in safety. And this is what he will be called: The LORD Is Our Righteousness.

1 Peter 1:13-21

Therefore, once you have your minds ready for action and you are thinking clearly, place your hope completely on the grace that will be brought to you when Jesus Christ is revealed. Don't be conformed to your former desires, those that shaped you when you were ignorant. But, as obedient children, you must be holy in every aspect of your lives, just as the one who called you is holy. It is written, *You will be holy, because I am holy*. Since you call upon a Father who judges all people according to their actions without favoritism, you should conduct yourselves with reverence during the time of your dwelling in a strange land. Live in this way, knowing that you were not liberated by perishable things like silver or gold from the empty lifestyle you inherited from your ancestors. Instead, you were liberated by the precious blood of Christ, like that of a flawless, spotless lamb. Christ was chosen before the creation of the world, but was only revealed at the end of time. This was done for you, who through Christ are faithful to the God who raised him from the dead and gave him glory. So now, your faith and hope should rest in God.

MEDITATION

Our faith and hope rest in the promises and faithfulness of God, and we look for signs of God's kingdom breaking forth. Where do you see signs of God's rule in effect in your life? In your community? In the world?

DAY 9

Psalm 96:1-4a, 11-13

Sing to the LORD a new song!
  Sing to the LORD, all the earth!
Sing to the LORD! Bless his name!
  Share the news of his saving work every single day!
Declare God's glory among the nations;
  declare his wondrous works among all people
  because the LORD is great and so worthy of praise.

Let heaven celebrate! Let the earth rejoice!
  Let the sea and everything in it roar!
  Let the countryside and everything in it celebrate!
  Then all the trees of the forest too
    will shout out joyfully
    before the LORD because he is coming!
He is coming to establish justice on the earth!
  He will establish justice in the world rightly.
  He will establish justice among all people fairly.

Matthew 9:9-13

As Jesus continued on from there, he saw a man named Matthew sitting at a kiosk for collecting taxes. He said to him, "Follow me," and he got up and followed him. As Jesus sat down to eat in Matthew's house, many tax collectors and sinners joined Jesus and his disciples at the table.

But when the Pharisees saw this, they said to his disciples, "Why does your teacher eat with tax collectors and sinners?"

When Jesus heard it, he said, "Healthy people don't need a doctor, but sick people do. Go and learn what this means: *I want mercy and not sacrifice.* I didn't come to call righteous people, but sinners."

Romans 8:18-25

I believe that the present suffering is nothing compared to the coming glory that is going to be revealed to us. The whole creation waits breathless with anticipation for the revelation of God's sons and daughters. Creation was subjected to frustration, not by its own choice—it was the choice of the one who subjected it—but in the hope that the creation itself will be set free from slavery to decay and brought into the glorious freedom of God's children. We know that the whole creation is groaning together and suffering labor pains up until now. And it's not only the creation. We ourselves who have the Spirit as the first crop of the harvest also groan inside as we wait to be adopted and for our bodies to be set free. We were saved in hope. If we see what we hope for, that isn't hope. Who hopes for what they already see? But if we hope for what we don't see, we wait for it with patience.

MEDITATION

Today's scriptures lead us to consider our hope of the healing of our bodies, our spirits, and indeed, even all of creation. Where do you see the need for healing, personally and communally? How are you cooperating with God in the healing of creation?

DAY 10

John 1:1-14

In the beginning was the Word
  and the Word was with God
  and the Word was God.
The Word was with God in the beginning.
Everything came into being through the Word,
  and without the Word
  nothing came into being.
What came into being
  through the Word was life,
  and the life was the light for all people.
The light shines in the darkness,
  and the darkness doesn't extinguish the light.
  A man named John was sent from God. He came as a witness to testify concerning the light, so that through him everyone would believe in the light. He himself wasn't the light, but his mission was to testify concerning the light.
The true light that shines on all people
  was coming into the world.
The light was in the world,
  and the world came into being through the light,
    but the world didn't recognize the light.
The light came to his own people,
  and his own people didn't welcome him.

But those who did welcome him,
    those who believed in his name,
  he authorized to become God's children,
    born not from blood
    nor from human desire or passion,
    but born from God.
The Word became flesh
  and made his home among us.
We have seen his glory,
  glory like that of a father's only son,
    full of grace and truth.

Isaiah 12:2

"God is indeed my salvation;
  I will trust and won't be afraid.
Yah, the LORD, is my strength and my shield;
  he has become my salvation."

Psalm 145:1-2, 13

I will lift you up high, my God, the true king.
  I will bless your name forever and always.
I will bless you every day.
  I will praise your name forever and always.
Your kingdom is a kingship that lasts forever;
  your rule endures for all generations.
The LORD is trustworthy in all that he says,
  faithful in all that he does.

MEDITATION

The prophet and psalmist trust God for their salvation, and the Gospel of John affirms that our salvation comes through Jesus Christ, "the light for all people." Name and give thanks for the ways you have seen the light of Christ shining in the darkness.

PEACE

DAY 11

Isaiah 11:1-10

A shoot will grow up from the stump of Jesse;
  a branch will sprout from his roots.
The LORD's spirit will rest upon him,
  a spirit of wisdom and understanding,
  a spirit of planning and strength,
  a spirit of knowledge and fear of the LORD.
He will delight in fearing the LORD.
He won't judge by appearances,
  nor decide by hearsay.
He will judge the needy with righteousness,
  and decide with equity for those who suffer in the land.
He will strike the violent with the rod of his mouth;
  by the breath of his lips he will kill the wicked.
Righteousness will be the belt around his hips,
  and faithfulness the belt around his waist.
The wolf will live with the lamb,
  and the leopard will lie down with the young goat;

the calf and the young lion will feed together,
and a little child will lead them.
The cow and the bear will graze.
Their young will lie down together,
and a lion will eat straw like an ox.
A nursing child will play over the snake's hole;
toddlers will reach right over the serpent's den.
They won't harm or destroy anywhere
on my holy mountain.
The earth will surely be filled
with the knowledge of the LORD,
just as the water covers the sea.

On that day, the root of Jesse will stand as a signal to the peoples. The nations will seek him out, and his dwelling will be glorious.

Luke 1:67-79

John's father Zechariah was filled with the Holy Spirit and prophesied,

"Bless the Lord God of Israel
because he has come to help
and has delivered his people.
He has raised up a mighty savior for us
in his servant David's house,
just as he said through the mouths
of his holy prophets long ago.
He has brought salvation from our enemies
and from the power of all those who hate us.
He has shown the mercy promised to our ancestors,
and remembered his holy covenant,

the solemn pledge he made to our ancestor Abraham.
He has granted that we would be rescued
  from the power of our enemies
  so that we could serve him without fear,
    in holiness and righteousness in God's eyes,
      for as long as we live.
You, child, will be called a prophet of the Most High,
  for you will go before the Lord to prepare his way.
You will tell his people how to be saved
  through the forgiveness of their sins.
Because of our God's deep compassion,
  the dawn from heaven will break upon us,
  to give light to those who are sitting in darkness
  and in the shadow of death,
    to guide us on the path of peace."

Psalm 106:48

Bless the LORD, the God of Israel,
  from forever ago to forever from now!
  And let all the people say, "Amen!"

Praise the LORD!

MEDITATION

*Isaiah looked forward to an idyllic ruler
in the line of David, a wise and just judge that
would bring peace to all creation. The priest
Zechariah praised God because God's ancient
promise was about to be fulfilled in the one
who would "guide us on the path of peace."
Where do you long for the righteousness
of God? For the compassion of God?
Where do you find peace?*

DAY 12

Malachi 3:1-4

Look, I am sending my messenger
  who will clear the path before me;
    suddenly the LORD whom you are seeking
      will come to his temple.
  The messenger of the covenant in whom
    you take delight is coming,
  says the LORD of heavenly forces.
Who can endure the day of his coming?
  Who can withstand his appearance?
He is like the refiner's fire or the cleaner's soap.
He will sit as a refiner and a purifier of silver.
  He will purify the Levites and refine them
    like gold and silver.
    They will belong to the LORD,
      presenting a righteous offering.
The offering of Judah and Jerusalem
  will be pleasing to the LORD
  as in ancient days and in former years.

Luke 3:2b-3

God's word came to John son of Zechariah in the wilderness. John went throughout the region of the Jordan River, calling for people to be baptized to show that they were changing their hearts and lives and wanted God to forgive their sins.

Psalm 51:1-13

Have mercy on me, God,
  according to your faithful love!
  Wipe away my wrongdoings
    according to your great compassion!
Wash me completely clean of my guilt;
  purify me from my sin!
Because I know my wrongdoings,
  my sin is always right in front of me.
I've sinned against you—you alone.
  I've committed evil in your sight.
That's why you are justified when you render
  your verdict,
  completely correct when you issue your judgment.
Yes, I was born in guilt, in sin,
  from the moment my mother conceived me.
And yes, you want truth in the most hidden places;
  you teach me wisdom in the most secret space.

Purify me with hyssop and I will be clean;
  wash me and I will be whiter than snow.

Let me hear joy and celebration again;
   let the bones you crushed rejoice once more.
Hide your face from my sins;
   wipe away all my guilty deeds!
Create a clean heart for me, God;
   put a new, faithful spirit deep inside me!
Please don't throw me out of your presence;
   please don't take your holy spirit away from me.
Return the joy of your salvation to me
   and sustain me with a willing spirit.
Then I will teach wrongdoers your ways,
   and sinners will come back to you.

MEDITATION

*These readings guide us in understanding
that peace with God involves confession of who
we are before God. Using Psalm 51 as a guide,
write your own prayer of confession.*

DAY 13

Matthew 3:1-12

In those days John the Baptist appeared in the desert of Judea announcing, "Change your hearts and lives! Here comes the kingdom of heaven!" He was the one of whom Isaiah the prophet spoke when he said:

The voice of one shouting in the wilderness,
"Prepare the way for the Lord;
make his paths straight."

John wore clothes made of camel's hair, with a leather belt around his waist. He ate locusts and wild honey.

People from Jerusalem, throughout Judea, and all around the Jordan River came to him. As they confessed their sins, he baptized them in the Jordan River. Many Pharisees and Sadducees came to be baptized by John. He said to them, "You children of snakes! Who warned you to escape from the angry judgment that is coming soon? Produce fruit that shows you have changed your hearts and lives. And don't even think about saying to yourselves, Abraham is our father. I tell you that God is able to raise up Abraham's children from these stones. The ax is already at the root of the trees. Therefore, every tree that doesn't produce good fruit will be chopped down and tossed into the fire. I baptize with water those of you who have changed your hearts and lives. The one who is coming after me is stronger than I am. I'm not worthy to carry his sandals. He will baptize you with the Holy Spirit and with fire. The shovel he uses to sift the wheat from the husks is in his hands. He will clean out his threshing area and bring the wheat into his barn. But he will burn the husks with a fire that can't be put out."

Psalm 130

I cry out to you from the depths, LORD—
  my Lord, listen to my voice!
  Let your ears pay close attention
    to my request for mercy!
If you kept track of sins, LORD—
  my Lord, who would stand a chance?
But forgiveness is with you—
  that's why you are honored.

I hope, LORD. My whole being hopes,
  and I wait for God's promise.
My whole being waits for my Lord—
  more than the night watch waits for morning;
  yes, more than the night watch waits for morning!

Israel, wait for the LORD!
  Because faithful love is with the LORD;
  because great redemption is with our God!
He is the one who will redeem Israel from all its sin.

Psalm 139:23-24

Examine me, God! Look at my heart!
 Put me to the test! Know my anxious thoughts!
Look to see if there is any idolatrous way in me,
 then lead me on the eternal path!

MEDITATION

*John the Baptist calls for changed lives
that will lead to restoration, and the psalmists
affirm God's power to forgive and transform
us. When have you seen or experienced
repentance that led to peace with God?
With family or friends? Is there an area
of your life that needs to be transformed
by the power of God?*

Day 14

Philippians 1:3-11

I thank my God every time I mention you in my prayers. I'm thankful for all of you every time I pray, and it's always a prayer full of joy. I'm glad because of the way you have been my partners in the ministry of the gospel from the time you first believed it until now. I'm sure about this: the one who started a good work in you will stay with you to complete the job by the day of Christ Jesus. I have good reason to think this way about all of you because I keep you in my heart. You are all my partners in God's grace, both during my time in prison and in the defense and support of the gospel. God is my witness that I feel affection for all of you with the compassion of Christ Jesus.

This is my prayer: that your love might become even more and more rich with knowledge and all kinds of insight. I pray this so that you will be able to decide what really matters and so you will be sincere and blameless on the day of Christ. I pray that you will then be filled with the fruit of righteousness, which comes from Jesus Christ, in order to give glory and praise to God.

Luke 2:39-51

When Mary and Joseph had completed everything required by the Law of the Lord, they returned to their hometown, Nazareth in Galilee. The child grew up and became strong. He was filled with wisdom, and God's favor was on him.

Each year his parents went to Jerusalem for the Passover Festival. When he was 12 years old, they went up to Jerusalem according to their custom. After the festival was over, they were returning home, but the boy Jesus stayed behind in Jerusalem. His parents didn't know it. Supposing that he was among their band of travelers, they journeyed on for a full day while looking for him among their family and friends. When they didn't find Jesus, they returned to Jerusalem to look for him. After three days they found him in the temple. He was sitting among the teachers, listening to them and putting questions to them. Everyone who heard him was amazed by his understanding and his answers. When his parents saw him, they were shocked.

His mother said, "Child, why have you treated us like this? Listen! Your father and I have been worried. We've been looking for you!"

Jesus replied, "Why were you looking for me? Didn't you know that it was necessary for me to be in my Father's house?" But they didn't understand what he said to them.

Jesus went down to Nazareth with them and was obedient to them. His mother cherished every word in her heart.

MEDITATION

*Paul prays that the Philippians will grow
in wisdom; that is, that they will grow in love
that is enriched with knowledge and insight.
How does knowing "what really matters"
bring us peace with God and neighbor?*

DAY 15

Romans 15:4-13

Whatever was written in the past was written for our instruction so that we could have hope through endurance and through the encouragement of the scriptures. May the God of endurance and encouragement give you the same attitude toward each other, similar to Christ Jesus' attitude. That way you can glorify the God and Father of our Lord Jesus Christ together with one voice.

So welcome each other, in the same way that Christ also welcomed you, for God's glory. I'm saying that Christ became a servant of those who are circumcised for the sake of God's truth, in order to confirm the promises given to the ancestors, and so that the Gentiles could glorify God for his mercy. As it is written,

Because of this I will confess you among the Gentiles,
  and I will sing praises to your name.
And again, it says,
Rejoice, Gentiles, with his people.
And again,
Praise the Lord, all you Gentiles,
  and all the people should sing his praises.
And again, Isaiah says,
There will be a root of Jesse,
  who will also rise to rule the Gentiles.
    The Gentiles will place their hope in him.

May the God of hope fill you with all joy and peace in faith so that you overflow with hope by the power of the Holy Spirit.

Ephesians 4:1-7, 11-16

Therefore, as a prisoner for the Lord, I encourage you to live as people worthy of the call you received from God. Conduct yourselves with all humility, gentleness, and patience. Accept each other with love, and make an effort to preserve the unity of the Spirit with the peace that ties you together. You are one body and one spirit, just as God also called you in one hope. There is one Lord, one faith, one baptism, and one God and Father of all, who is over all, through all, and in all.

God has given his grace to each one of us measured out by the gift that is given by Christ. He gave some apostles, some prophets, some evangelists, and some pastors and teachers. His purpose was to equip God's people for the work of serving and building up the body of Christ until we all reach the unity of faith and knowledge of God's Son. God's goal is for us to become mature adults—to be fully grown, measured by the standard of the fullness of Christ. As a result, we aren't supposed to be infants any longer who can be tossed and blown around by every wind that comes from teaching with deceitful scheming and the tricks people play to deliberately mislead others. Instead, by speaking the truth with love, let's grow in every way into Christ, who is the head. The whole body grows from him, as it is joined and held together by all the supporting ligaments. The body makes itself grow in that it builds itself up with love as each one does their part.

MEDITATION

In these letters, Paul describes the foundation of life in Christian community—just as God welcomes all in love, we are to extend God's love to all in the hope of unity. What are the obstacles to living in unity in Christian community? How are you and your faith community working toward unity in the body of Christ?

Day 16

Psalm 72:1-7, 12-14, 18-19

God, give your judgments to the king.
  Give your righteousness to the king's son.
Let him judge your people with righteousness
  and your poor ones with justice.
Let the mountains bring peace to the people;
  let the hills bring righteousness.
Let the king bring justice to people who are poor;
  let him save the children of those who are needy,
    but let him crush oppressors!
Let the king live as long as the sun,
  as long as the moon, generation to generation.
Let him fall like rain upon fresh-cut grass,
  like showers that water the earth.
Let the righteous flourish throughout their lives,
  and let peace prosper until the moon is no more.

Let it be so, because he delivers the needy who cry out,
  the poor, and those who have no helper.
He has compassion on the weak and the needy;
  he saves the lives of those who are in need.
He redeems their lives from oppression and violence;
  their blood is precious in his eyes.

Bless the LORD God, the God of Israel—
  the only one who does wondrous things!
Bless God's glorious name forever;
  let his glory fill all the earth!
Amen and Amen!

Romans 12:9-21

Love should be shown without pretending. Hate evil, and hold on to what is good. Love each other like the members of your family. Be the best at showing honor to each other. Don't hesitate to be enthusiastic—be on fire in the Spirit as you serve the Lord! Be happy in your hope, stand your ground when you're in trouble, and devote yourselves to prayer. Contribute to the needs of God's people, and welcome strangers into your home. Bless people who harass you—bless and don't curse them. Be happy with those who are happy, and cry with those who are crying. Consider everyone as equal, and don't think that you're better than anyone else. Instead, associate with people who have no status. Don't think that you're so smart. Don't pay back anyone for their evil actions with evil actions, but show respect for what everyone else believes is good.

If possible, to the best of your ability, live at peace with all people. Don't try to get revenge for yourselves, my dear friends, but leave room for God's wrath. It is written, *Revenge belongs to me; I will pay it back, says the Lord.* Instead, *If your enemy is hungry, feed him; if he is thirsty, give him a drink. By doing this, you will pile burning coals of fire upon his head.* Don't be defeated by evil, but defeat evil with good.

Matthew 5:9

"Happy are people who make peace, because they will be called God's children."

~ **MEDITATION** ~

*The psalmist longs for a king that
will bring justice to the poor, save the
children of the needy, and bring peace.
Paul urges the Christian community
to "defeat evil with good." What do we look
for in our leaders? Write a prayer for the
leaders of your faith community
and for the leaders of the world.*

DAY 17

2 Peter 3:8-15

Don't let it escape your notice, dear friends, that with the Lord a single day is like a thousand years and a thousand years are like a single day. The Lord isn't slow to keep his promise, as some think of slowness, but he is patient toward you, not wanting anyone to perish but all to change their hearts and lives. But the day of the Lord will come like a thief. On that day the heavens will pass away with a dreadful noise, the elements will be consumed by fire, and the earth and all the works done on it will be exposed.

Since everything will be destroyed in this way, what sort of people ought you to be? You must live holy and godly lives, waiting for and hastening the coming day of God. Because of that day, the heavens will be destroyed by fire and the elements will melt away in the flames. But according to his promise we are waiting for a new heaven and a new earth, where righteousness is at home.

Therefore, dear friends, while you are waiting for these things to happen, make every effort to be found by him in peace—pure and faultless. Consider the patience of our Lord to be salvation, just as our dear friend and brother Paul wrote to you according to the wisdom given to him.

Colossians 3:12-17

Therefore, as God's choice, holy and loved, put on compassion, kindness, humility, gentleness, and patience. Be tolerant with each other and, if someone has a complaint against anyone, forgive each other. As the Lord forgave you, so also forgive each other. And over all these things put on love, which is the perfect bond of unity. The peace of Christ must control your hearts—a peace into which you were called in one body. And be thankful people. The word of Christ must live in you richly. Teach and warn each other with all wisdom by singing psalms, hymns, and spiritual songs. Sing to God with gratitude in your hearts. Whatever you do, whether in speech or action, do it all in the name of the Lord Jesus and give thanks to God the Father through him.

1 Corinthians 13:4-13

Love is patient, love is kind, it isn't jealous, it doesn't brag, it isn't arrogant, it isn't rude, it doesn't seek its own advantage, it isn't irritable, it doesn't keep a record of complaints, it isn't happy with injustice, but it is happy with the truth. Love puts up with all things, trusts in all things, hopes for all things, endures all things.

Love never fails. As for prophecies, they will be brought to an end. As for tongues, they will stop. As for knowledge, it will be brought to an end. We know in part and we prophesy in part; but when the perfect comes, what is partial will be brought to an end. When I was a child, I used to speak like a child, reason like a child, think like a child. But now that I have become a man, I've put an end to childish things. Now we see a reflection in a mirror; then we will see face-to-face. Now I know partially, but then I will know completely in the same way that I have been completely known. Now faith, hope, and love remain—these three things—and the greatest of these is love.

MEDITATION

These New Testament letters affirm
God's patience in judgment, desiring that
all will change their hearts and lives,
and they proclaim patience as crucial to life
in Christian community, for "love is patient."
Reflect on how patience may lead to peace
in your life—in your family, with your friends,
and in your community of faith.

DAY 18

Isaiah 40:1-5

Comfort, comfort my people! says your God.
Speak compassionately to Jerusalem,
    and proclaim to her that her compulsory service
        has ended,
that her penalty has been paid,
that she has received from the LORD's hand double
    for all her sins!

A voice is crying out:
"Clear the LORD's way in the desert!
    Make a level highway in the wilderness for our God!
Every valley will be raised up,
    and every mountain and hill will be flattened.
    Uneven ground will become level,
    and rough terrain a valley plain.
The LORD's glory will appear,
    and all humanity will see it together;
    the LORD's mouth has commanded it."

Psalm 46

God is our refuge and strength,
  a help always near in times of great trouble.
That's why we won't be afraid
  when the world falls apart,
  when the mountains crumble
    into the center of the sea,
  when its waters roar and rage,
  when the mountains shake
    because of its surging waves.

There is a river whose streams gladden God's city,
  the holiest dwelling of the Most High.
God is in that city. It will never crumble.
  God will help it when morning dawns.
Nations roar; kingdoms crumble.
  God utters his voice; the earth melts.
The LORD of heavenly forces is with us!
  The God of Jacob is our place of safety.

Come, see the LORD's deeds,
  what devastation he has imposed on the earth—
  bringing wars to an end in every corner of the world,
  breaking the bow and shattering the spear,
    burning chariots with fire.

"That's enough! Now know that I am God!
  I am exalted among all nations;
    I am exalted throughout the world!"

The LORD of heavenly forces is with us!
  The God of Jacob is our place of safety.

MEDITATION

Today's readings celebrate that God has saved God's people in the past, God is saving us now, and God will save in the future. How have you experience salvation in the past? How is God saving you now? In what ways do you look forward to God's future salvation?

DAY 19

Mark 1:1-8

The beginning of the good news about Jesus Christ, God's Son, happened just as it was written about in the prophecy of Isaiah:

Look, I am sending my messenger before you.
He will prepare your way,
a voice shouting in the wilderness:
　"Prepare the way for the Lord;
　make his paths straight."

John the Baptist was in the wilderness calling for people to be baptized to show that they were changing their hearts and lives and wanted God to forgive their sins. Everyone in Judea and all the people of Jerusalem went out to the Jordan River and were being baptized by John as they confessed their sins. John wore clothes made of camel's hair, with a leather belt around his waist. He ate locusts and wild honey. He announced, "One stronger than I am is coming after me. I'm not even worthy to bend over and loosen the strap of his sandals. I baptize you with water, but he will baptize you with the Holy Spirit."

Matthew 25:31-40

"Now when the Human One comes in his majesty and all his angels are with him, he will sit on his majestic throne. All the nations will be gathered in front of him. He will separate them from each other, just as a shepherd separates the sheep from the goats. He will put the sheep on his right side. But the goats he will put on his left.

"Then the king will say to those on his right, 'Come, you who will receive good things from my Father. Inherit the kingdom that was prepared for you before the world began. I was hungry and you gave me food to eat. I was thirsty and you gave me a drink. I was a stranger and you welcomed me. I was naked and you gave me clothes to wear. I was sick and you took care of me. I was in prison and you visited me.'

"Then those who are righteous will reply to him, 'Lord, when did we see you hungry and feed you, or thirsty and give you a drink? When did we see you as a stranger and welcome you, or naked and give you clothes to wear? When did we see you sick or in prison and visit you?'

"Then the king will reply to them, 'I assure you that when you have done it for one of the least of these brothers and sisters of mine, you have done it for me.'"

John 14:1-7

"Don't be troubled. Trust in God. Trust also in me. My Father's house has room to spare. If that weren't the case, would I have told you that I'm going to prepare a place for you? When I go to prepare a place for you, I will return and take you to be with me so that where I am you will be too. You know the way to the place I'm going."

Thomas asked, "Lord, we don't know where you are going. How can we know the way?"

Jesus answered, "I am the way, the truth, and the life. No one comes to the Father except through me. If you have really known me, you will also know the Father. From now on you know him and have seen him."

MEDITATION

John the Baptist prepared the way for Jesus. Jesus prepared the kingdom for us, and we enter with acts of compassion and love, empowered by the Spirit. Who prepared the way for you in your life in Christ? Give thanks for them. Which people might you be helping to prepare for a life in the kingdom?

Day 20

Isaiah 9:2-7

The people walking in darkness have seen a great light.
  On those living in a pitch-dark land, light has dawned.
You have made the nation great;
  you have increased its joy.
They rejoiced before you as with joy at the harvest,
  as those who divide plunder rejoice.
As on the day of Midian,
  you've shattered the yoke that burdened them,
  the staff on their shoulders,
  and the rod of their oppressor.
Because every boot of the thundering warriors,
  and every garment rolled in blood will be burned,
    fuel for the fire.
A child is born to us, a son is given to us,
  and authority will be on his shoulders.
  He will be named Wonderful Counselor, Mighty God,
    Eternal Father, Prince of Peace.
There will be vast authority and endless peace
  for David's throne and for his kingdom,
  establishing and sustaining it
    with justice and righteousness
  now and forever.
The zeal of the LORD of heavenly forces will do this.

Psalm 98

Sing to the LORD a new song
  because he has done wonderful things!
His own strong hand and his own holy arm
  have won the victory!
The LORD has made his salvation widely known;
  he has revealed his righteousness in the eyes
    of all the nations.
God has remembered his loyal love and faithfulness
  to the house of Israel;
    every corner of the earth
      has seen our God's salvation.

Shout triumphantly to the LORD, all the earth!
  Be happy!
  Rejoice out loud!
  Sing your praises!
Sing your praises to the LORD with the lyre—
  with the lyre and the sound of music.
With trumpets and a horn blast,
  shout triumphantly before the LORD, the king!
Let the sea and everything in it roar;
  the world and all its inhabitants too.
Let all the rivers clap their hands;
  let the mountains rejoice out loud altogether
    before the LORD
  because he is coming to establish justice on the earth!
He will establish justice in the world rightly;
  he will establish justice among all people fairly.

Luke 2:25-35

A man named Simeon was in Jerusalem. He was righteous and devout. He eagerly anticipated the restoration of Israel, and the Holy Spirit rested on him. The Holy Spirit revealed to him that he wouldn't die before he had seen the Lord's Christ. Led by the Spirit, he went into the temple area. Meanwhile, Jesus' parents brought the child to the temple so that they could do what was customary under the Law. Simeon took Jesus in his arms and praised God. He said,

"Now, master, let your servant go in peace
according to your word,
because my eyes have seen your salvation.
You prepared this salvation in the presence
of all peoples.
It's a light for revelation to the Gentiles
and a glory for your people Israel."

His father and mother were amazed by what was said about him. Simeon blessed them and said to Mary his mother, "This boy is assigned to be the cause of the falling and rising of many in Israel and to be a sign that generates opposition so that the inner thoughts of many will be revealed. And a sword will pierce your innermost being too."

MEDITATION

*The Christmas Eve reading from Isaiah
celebrates a future king that will bring peace
and justice to the nations, and the Christmas
Day reading of Psalm 98 praises God's mighty
deeds. In Luke, the song of the prophet Simeon
captures the joy and peace of one who has
witnessed God's salvation in the birth of Jesus.
What mighty deeds of God do you celebrate
today? Where have you experienced the joy
and peace that come from witnessing
God's salvation for all people?*

J O Y

DAY 21

Isaiah 35:1-7

The desert and the dry land will be glad;
  the wilderness will rejoice and blossom like the crocus.
They will burst into bloom,
  and rejoice with joy and singing.
They will receive the glory of Lebanon,
  the splendor of Carmel and Sharon.
They will see the LORD's glory,
  the splendor of our God.

Strengthen the weak hands,
  and support the unsteady knees.
Say to those who are panicking:
  "Be strong! Don't fear!
  Here's your God, coming with vengeance;
    with divine retribution God will come to save you."

Then the eyes of the blind will be opened,
   and the ears of the deaf will be cleared.
Then the lame will leap like the deer,
   and the tongue of the speechless will sing.
Waters will spring up in the desert,
   and streams in the wilderness.
The burning sand will become a pool,
   and the thirsty ground, fountains of water.
The jackals' habitat, a pasture;
   grass will become reeds and rushes.

Revelation 21:1-6

Then I saw a new heaven and a new earth, for the former heaven and the former earth had passed away, and the sea was no more. I saw the holy city, New Jerusalem, coming down out of heaven from God, made ready as a bride beautifully dressed for her husband. I heard a loud voice from the throne say, "Look! God's dwelling is here with humankind. He will dwell with them, and they will be his peoples. God himself will be with them as their God. He will wipe away every tear from their eyes. Death will be no more. There will be no mourning, crying, or pain anymore, for the former things have passed away." Then the one seated on the throne said, "Look! I'm making all things new." He also said, "Write this down, for these words are trustworthy and true." Then he said to me, "All is done. I am the Alpha and the Omega, the beginning and the end. To the thirsty I will freely give water from the life-giving spring."

MEDITATION

*Through God's gracious power the wilderness
is turned into fertile land, says Isaiah.
John has a vision that eventually the whole
earth will become a new creation,
and there will be the joy of a new creation—
for individuals, for peoples, for the land.
What is your vision of the new creation?*

DAY 22

Psalm 146

Praise the LORD!

Let my whole being praise the LORD!
I will praise the LORD with all my life;
   I will sing praises to my God as long as I live.

Don't trust leaders; don't trust any human beings—
   there's no saving help with them!
Their breath leaves them,
   then they go back to the ground.
   On that very same day, their plans die too.

The person whose help is the God of Jacob—
   the person whose hope rests on the LORD their God—
      is truly happy!
God: the maker of heaven and earth, the sea,
   and all that is in them,
God: who is faithful forever,
   who gives justice to people who are oppressed,
   who gives bread to people who are starving!
The LORD: who frees prisoners.
   The LORD: who makes the blind see.
   The LORD: who straightens up those who are bent low.

The LORD: who loves the righteous.
The LORD: who protects immigrants,
   who helps orphans and widows,
      but who makes the way of the wicked
         twist and turn!

The LORD will rule forever!
   Zion, your God will rule
      from one generation to the next!

Praise the LORD!

Luke 18:1-8

Jesus was telling them a parable about their need to pray continuously and not to be discouraged. He said, "In a certain city there was a judge who neither feared God nor respected people. In that city there was a widow who kept coming to him, asking, 'Give me justice in this case against my adversary.' For a while he refused but finally said to himself, I don't fear God or respect people, but I will give this widow justice because she keeps bothering me. Otherwise, there will be no end to her coming here and embarrassing me." The Lord said, "Listen to what the unjust judge says. Won't God provide justice to his chosen people who cry out to him day and night? Will he be slow to help them? I tell you, he will give them justice quickly. But when the Human One comes, will he find faithfulness on earth?"

MEDITATION

God, the faithful Creator, wants justice for the people of the earth, especially those without food, freedom, power, or health. God provides justice, says the psalmist, and in Luke, Jesus affirms this and includes himself as a faithful provider of justice. Who are the vulnerable and powerless in our world today? Name them. How can we responsibly use power to respond to those on the margins of society?

DAY 23

James 5:7-10

Therefore, brothers and sisters, you must be patient as you wait for the coming of the Lord. Consider the farmer who waits patiently for the coming of rain in the fall and spring, looking forward to the precious fruit of the earth. You also must wait patiently, strengthening your resolve, because the coming of the Lord is near. Don't complain about each other, brothers and sisters, so that you won't be judged. Look! The judge is standing at the door!

Brothers and sisters, take the prophets who spoke in the name of the Lord as an example of patient resolve and steadfastness.

Romans 5:1-11

Therefore, since we have been made righteous through his faithfulness, we have peace with God through our Lord Jesus Christ. We have access by faith into this grace in which we stand through him, and we boast in the hope of God's glory. But not only that! We even take pride in our problems, because we know that trouble produces endurance, endurance produces character, and character produces hope. This hope doesn't put us to shame, because the love of God has been poured out in our hearts through the Holy Spirit, who has been given to us.

While we were still weak, at the right moment, Christ died for ungodly people. It isn't often that someone will die for a righteous person, though maybe someone might dare to die for a good person. But God shows his love for us, because while we were still sinners Christ died for us. So, now that we have been made righteous by his blood, we can be even more certain that we will be saved from God's wrath through him. If we were reconciled to God through the death of his Son while we were still enemies, now that we have been reconciled, how much more certain is it that we will be saved by his life? And not only that: we even take pride in God through our Lord Jesus Christ, the one through whom we now have a restored relationship with God.

Psalm 118:1-4

Give thanks to the LORD because he is good,
   because his faithful love lasts forever.
Let Israel say it:
   "God's faithful love lasts forever!"
Let the house of Aaron say it:
   "God's faithful love lasts forever!"
Let those who honor the LORD say it:
   "God's faithful love lasts forever!"

MEDITATION

Early Christians affirmed that faith in Christ does not exempt Christians from suffering, and they also affirmed the virtue of patient endurance during times of suffering. We can endure because "God's faithful love lasts forever." Though we never welcome suffering, we may have witnessed or experienced a truth in Paul's faith statement that suffering in Christ leads to endurance, which forms character, which produces hope. What feelings arise in you when you hear that statement? What questions does it bring for you, especially as we consider suffering in relationship to joy?

DAY 24

Isaiah 61:1-4, 8-9

The LORD God's spirit is upon me,
  because the LORD has anointed me.
He has sent me
  to bring good news to the poor,
  to bind up the brokenhearted,
  to proclaim release for captives,
    and liberation for prisoners,
  to proclaim the year of the LORD's favor
    and a day of vindication for our God,
  to comfort all who mourn,
  to provide for Zion's mourners,
  to give them a crown in place of ashes,
  oil of joy in place of mourning,
  a mantle of praise in place of discouragement.
They will be called Oaks of Righteousness,
  planted by the LORD to glorify himself.
They will rebuild the ancient ruins;
  they will restore formerly deserted places;
  they will renew ruined cities,
  places deserted in generations past.

I, the LORD, love justice;
  I hate robbery and dishonesty.

I will faithfully give them their wage,
   and make with them an enduring covenant.
Their offspring will be known among the nations,
   and their descendants among the peoples.
All who see them will recognize that they are a people
   blessed by the LORD.

Matthew 11:2-11

Now when John heard in prison about the things the Christ was doing, he sent word by his disciples to Jesus, asking, "Are you the one who is to come, or should we look for another?"

Jesus responded, "Go, report to John what you hear and see. *Those who were blind are able to see.* Those who were crippled are walking. People with skin diseases are cleansed. Those *who were deaf now hear. Those who were dead are raised up. The poor have good news proclaimed to them.* Happy are those who don't stumble and fall because of me."

When John's disciples had gone, Jesus spoke to the crowds about John: "What did you go out to the wilderness to see? A stalk blowing in the wind? What did you go out to see? A man dressed up in refined clothes? Look, those who wear refined clothes are in royal palaces. What did you go out to see? A prophet? Yes, I tell you, and more than a prophet. He is the one of whom it is written: *Look, I'm sending my messenger before you, who will prepare your way before you.*

"I assure you that no one who has ever been born is greater than John the Baptist. Yet whoever is least in the kingdom of heaven is greater than he."

MEDITATION

*The scriptures consistently tell us that God—
Creator, Son, and Holy Spirit—brings liberty
and release, but we are often tempted to ask,
like John the Baptist, "Should we look for
another?" Where do we look for our liberty?
Our security? Describe the type of joy
that comes from trust in God.*

Day 25

Psalm 126

When the LORD changed Zion's circumstances
  for the better,
  it was like we had been dreaming.
Our mouths were suddenly filled with laughter;
  our tongues were filled with joyful shouts.
It was even said, at that time, among the nations,
  "The LORD has done great things for them!"
Yes, the LORD has done great things for us,
  and we are overjoyed.

LORD, change our circumstances for the better,
  like dry streams in the desert waste!
Let those who plant with tears
  reap the harvest with joyful shouts.
Let those who go out, crying and carrying their seed,
  come home with joyful shouts,
    carrying bales of grain!

Acts 2:42-47

The believers devoted themselves to the apostles' teaching, to the community, to their shared meals, and to their prayers. A sense of awe came over everyone. God performed many wonders and signs through the apostles. All the believers were united and shared everything. They would sell pieces of property and possessions and distribute the proceeds to everyone who needed them. Every day, they met together in the temple and ate in their homes. They shared food with gladness and simplicity. They praised God and demonstrated God's goodness to everyone. The Lord added daily to the community those who were being saved.

1 Peter 2:1-10

Therefore, get rid of all ill will and all deceit, pretense, envy, and slander. Instead, like a newborn baby, desire the pure milk of the word. Nourished by it, you will grow into salvation, since you have tasted that the Lord is good.

Now you are coming to him as to a living stone. Even though this stone was rejected by humans, from God's perspective it is chosen, valuable. You yourselves are being built like living stones into a spiritual temple. You are being made into a holy priesthood to offer up spiritual sacrifices that are acceptable to God through Jesus Christ. Thus it is written in scripture, *Look! I am laying a cornerstone in Zion, chosen, valuable. The person who believes in him will never be shamed.* So God honors you who believe. For those who refuse to believe, though, the stone the builders tossed aside has become the capstone. This is a stone that makes people stumble and a rock that makes them fall. Because they refuse to believe in the word, they stumble. Indeed, this is the end to which they were appointed. But you are a chosen race, a royal priesthood, a holy nation, a people who are God's own possession. You have become this people so that you may speak of the wonderful acts of the one who called you out of darkness into his amazing light. Once you weren't a people, but now you are God's people. Once you hadn't received mercy, but now you have received mercy.

MEDITATION

Our readings today emphasize the joy
of a faith community that knows that one
of its purposes is to provide a witness to the
world of God's power, goodness, and mercy.
How does your church find joy in witnessing
to the "wonderful acts of the one who called
you out of darkness into his amazing light"?
Do you regularly exhibit the witness
of forgiveness? Of inclusiveness?

DAY 26

1 Thessalonians 5:16-24

Rejoice always. Pray continually. Give thanks in every situation because this is God's will for you in Christ Jesus. Don't suppress the Spirit. Don't brush off Spirit-inspired messages, but examine everything carefully and hang on to what is good. Avoid every kind of evil. Now, may the God of peace himself cause you to be completely dedicated to him; and may your spirit, soul, and body be kept intact and blameless at our Lord Jesus Christ's coming. The one who is calling you is faithful and will do this.

Philippians 4:4-7

Be glad in the Lord always! Again I say, be glad! Let your gentleness show in your treatment of all people. The Lord is near. Don't be anxious about anything; rather, bring up all of your requests to God in your prayers and petitions, along with giving thanks. Then the peace of God that exceeds all understanding will keep your hearts and minds safe in Christ Jesus.

Matthew 6:7-14

"When you pray, don't pour out a flood of empty words, as the Gentiles do. They think that by saying many words they'll be heard. Don't be like them, because your Father knows what you need before you ask. Pray like this:

Our Father who is in heaven,
　uphold the holiness of your name.
Bring in your kingdom
　so that your will is done on earth
　　as it's done in heaven.
Give us the bread we need for today.
Forgive us for the ways we have wronged you,
　just as we also forgive those who have wronged us.
And don't lead us into temptation,
　but rescue us from the evil one.

"If you forgive others their sins, your heavenly Father will also forgive you."

Psalm 65:1-3

God of Zion, to you even silence is praise.
　Promises made to you are kept—
　you listen to prayer—
　　and all living things come to you.
When wrongdoings become too much for me,
　you forgive our sins.

MEDITATION

*What are your prayers of thanksgiving
this day? Over what are you rejoicing?
What are your petitions today?*

DAY 27

John 1:6-8, 19-28

A man named John was sent from God. He came as a witness to testify concerning the light, so that through him everyone would believe in the light. He himself wasn't the light, but his mission was to testify concerning the light.

This is John's testimony when the Jewish leaders in Jerusalem sent priests and Levites to ask him, "Who are you?"

John confessed (he didn't deny but confessed), "I'm not the Christ."

They asked him, "Then who are you? Are you Elijah?"

John said, "I'm not."

"Are you the prophet?"

John answered, "No."

They asked, "Who are you? We need to give an answer to those who sent us. What do you say about yourself?"

John replied,

"*I am a voice crying out in the wilderness,*
    Make the Lord's path straight,

just as the prophet Isaiah said."

Those sent by the Pharisees asked, "Why do you baptize if you aren't the Christ, nor Elijah, nor the prophet?"

John answered, "I baptize with water. Someone greater stands among you, whom you don't recognize. He comes after me, but I'm not worthy to untie his sandal straps."

This encounter took place across the Jordan in Bethany where John was baptizing.

Luke 3:7-18

Then John said to the crowds who came to be baptized by him, "You children of snakes! Who warned you to escape from the angry judgment that is coming soon? Produce fruit that shows you have changed your hearts and lives. And don't even think about saying to yourselves, Abraham is our father. I tell you that God is able to raise up Abraham's children from these stones. The ax is already at the root of the trees. Therefore, every tree that doesn't produce good fruit will be chopped down and tossed into the fire."

The crowds asked him, "What then should we do?"

He answered, "Whoever has two shirts must share with the one who has none, and whoever has food must do the same."

Even tax collectors came to be baptized. They said to him, "Teacher, what should we do?"

He replied, "Collect no more than you are authorized to collect."

Soldiers asked, "What about us? What should we do?"

He answered, "Don't cheat or harass anyone, and be satisfied with your pay."

The people were filled with expectation, and everyone wondered whether John might be the Christ. John replied to them all, "I baptize you with water, but the one who is more powerful than me is coming. I'm not worthy to loosen the strap of his sandals. He will baptize you with the Holy

Spirit and fire. The shovel he uses to sift the wheat from the husks is in his hands. He will clean out his threshing area and bring the wheat into his barn. But he will burn the husks with a fire that can't be put out." With many other words John appealed to them, proclaiming good news to the people.

MEDITATION

John the Baptist is an example of one who knows what God has called him to do and responds with obedience. He points to Jesus, requiring those that would be baptized to produce good fruit—to live honestly in community and to share with one another. What fruit are you producing that leads to the joy of living peaceably in community? In what ways are you pointing to Jesus?

DAY 28

Zephaniah 3:14-19

Rejoice, Daughter Zion! Shout, Israel!
  Rejoice and exult with all your heart,
    Daughter Jerusalem.
The LORD has removed your judgment;
  he has turned away your enemy.
The LORD, the king of Israel, is in your midst;
  you will no longer fear evil.
On that day, it will be said to Jerusalem:
  Don't fear, Zion.
  Don't let your hands fall.
The LORD your God is in your midst—
  a warrior bringing victory.
  He will create calm with his love;
  he will rejoice over you with singing.

I will remove from you those worried
  about the appointed feasts.
They have been a burden for her, a reproach.
Watch what I am about to do to all your oppressors
  at that time.
  I will deliver the lame;
  I will gather the outcast.

> I will change their shame into praise and fame
> throughout the earth.

Luke 12:22-34

Then Jesus said to his disciples, "Therefore, I say to you, don't worry about your life, what you will eat, or about your body, what you will wear. There is more to life than food and more to the body than clothing. Consider the ravens: they neither plant nor harvest, they have no silo or barn, yet God feeds them. You are worth so much more than birds! Who among you by worrying can add a single moment to your life? If you can't do such a small thing, why worry about the rest? Notice how the lilies grow. They don't wear themselves out with work, and they don't spin cloth. But I say to you that even Solomon in all his splendor wasn't dressed like one of these. If God dresses grass in the field so beautifully, even though it's alive today and tomorrow it's thrown into the furnace, how much more will God do for you, you people of weak faith! Don't chase after what you will eat and what you will drink. Stop worrying. All the nations of the world long for these things. Your Father knows that you need them. Instead, desire his kingdom and these things will be given to you as well.

"Don't be afraid, little flock, because your Father delights in giving you the kingdom. Sell your possessions and give to those in need. Make for yourselves wallets that don't wear out—a treasure in heaven that never runs out. No thief comes near there, and no moth destroys. Where your treasure is, there your heart will be too."

MEDITATION

*God invites us to bring our anxieties to
the one who loves us enough to rejoice over
us with singing. What worries do you bring
to God today? What steps can you take
to become more obedient to Jesus' instruction:
"Don't worry"?*

DAY 29

Luke 2:1-20

In those days Caesar Augustus declared that everyone throughout the empire should be enrolled in the tax lists. This first enrollment occurred when Quirinius governed Syria. Everyone went to their own cities to be enrolled. Since Joseph belonged to David's house and family line, he went up from the city of Nazareth in Galilee to David's city, called Bethlehem, in Judea. He went to be enrolled together with Mary, who was promised to him in marriage and who was pregnant. While they were there, the time came for Mary to have her baby. She gave birth to her firstborn child, a son, wrapped him snugly, and laid him in a manger, because there was no place for them in the guestroom.

Nearby shepherds were living in the fields, guarding their sheep at night. The Lord's angel stood before them, the Lord's glory shone around them, and they were terrified.

The angel said, "Don't be afraid! Look! I bring good news to you—wonderful, joyous news for all people. Your savior is born today in David's city. He is Christ the Lord. This is a sign for you: you will find a newborn baby wrapped snugly and lying in a manger." Suddenly a great assembly of the heavenly forces was with the angel praising God. They said, "Glory to God in heaven, and on earth peace among those whom he favors."

When the angels returned to heaven, the shepherds said to each other, "Let's go right now to Bethlehem and see what's happened. Let's confirm what the Lord has revealed to us." They went quickly and found Mary and Joseph, and the baby lying in the manger. When they saw this, they reported what they had been told about this child. Everyone who heard it was amazed at what the shepherds told them. Mary committed these things to memory and considered them carefully. The shepherds returned home, glorifying and praising God for all they had heard and seen. Everything happened just as they had been told.

Matthew 28:1-10

After the Sabbath, at dawn on the first day of the week, Mary Magdalene and the other Mary came to look at the tomb. Look, there was a great earthquake, for an angel from the Lord came down from heaven. Coming to the stone, he rolled it away and sat on it. Now his face was like lightning and his clothes as white as snow. The guards were so terrified of him that they shook with fear and became like dead men. But the angel said to the women, "Don't be afraid. I know that you are looking for Jesus who was crucified. He isn't here, because he's been raised from the dead, just as he said. Come, see the place where they laid him. Now hurry, go and tell his disciples, 'He's been raised from the dead. He's going on ahead of you to Galilee. You will see him there.' I've given the message to you."

With great fear and excitement, they hurried away from the tomb and ran to tell his disciples. But Jesus met them and greeted them. They came and grabbed his feet and worshipped him. Then Jesus said to them, "Don't be afraid. Go and tell my brothers that I am going into Galilee. They will see me there."

MEDITATION

*Fear, amazement, surprise—these were
the experiences of the shepherds
at the birth of Jesus and of the two Marys
at the resurrection. When has the gospel
message birthed these experiences in you?*

DAY 30

Isaiah 52:7-10

How beautiful upon the mountains
  are the feet of a messenger
  who proclaims peace,
  who brings good news,
  who proclaims salvation,
  who says to Zion, "Your God rules!"
Listen! Your lookouts lift their voice;
  they sing out together!
  Right before their eyes they see the LORD
    returning to Zion.

Break into song together, you ruins of Jerusalem!
The LORD has comforted his people
  and has redeemed Jerusalem.
The LORD has bared his holy arm
  in view of all the nations;
  all the ends of the earth
    have seen our God's victory.

1 Corinthians 1:18-31

The message of the cross is foolishness to those who are being destroyed. But it is the power of God for those of us who are being saved. It is written in scripture: *I will destroy the wisdom of the wise, and I will reject the intelligence of the intelligent.* Where are the wise? Where are the legal experts? Where are today's debaters? Hasn't God made the wisdom of the world foolish? In God's wisdom, he determined that the world wouldn't come to know him through its wisdom. Instead, God was pleased to save those who believe through the foolishness of preaching. Jews ask for signs, and Greeks look for wisdom, but we preach Christ crucified, which is a scandal to Jews and foolishness to Gentiles. But to those who are called—both Jews and Greeks—Christ is God's power and God's wisdom. This is because the foolishness of God is wiser than human wisdom, and the weakness of God is stronger than human strength.

Look at your situation when you were called, brothers and sisters! By ordinary human standards not many were wise, not many were powerful, not many were from the upper class. But God chose what the world considers fool-ish to shame the wise. God chose what the world considers weak to shame the strong. And God chose what the world considers low-class and low-life—what is considered to be nothing—to reduce what is considered to be something to nothing. So no human being can brag in God's presence. It is because of God that you are in Christ Jesus. He became wisdom from God for us. This means that he made us righteous and holy, and he delivered us. This is consistent with what was written: *The one who brags should brag in the Lord!*

MEDITATION

The power of God that liberated the people of God from the rule of Babylon is the power now found in Christ Jesus, for "Christ is God's power and God's wisdom." Where do you see the power of Christ working in individual lives? How does God's wisdom sometimes seem like foolishness to the world?

LOVE

DAY 31

Matthew 1:18-25

This is how the birth of Jesus Christ took place. When Mary his mother was engaged to Joseph, before they were married, she became pregnant by the Holy Spirit. Joseph her husband was a righteous man. Because he didn't want to humiliate her, he decided to call off their engagement quietly. As he was thinking about this, an angel from the Lord appeared to him in a dream and said, "Joseph son of David, don't be afraid to take Mary as your wife, because the child she carries was conceived by the Holy Spirit. She will give birth to a son, and you will call him Jesus, because he will save his people from their sins." Now all of this took place so that what the Lord had spoken through the prophet would be fulfilled:

Look! A virgin will become pregnant
and give birth to a son,
And they will call him, Emmanuel.

(*Emmanuel* means "God with us.")

When Joseph woke up, he did just as an angel from God commanded and took Mary as his wife. But he didn't have sexual relations with her until she gave birth to a son. Joseph called him Jesus.

Luke 1:26-38

When Elizabeth was six months pregnant, God sent the angel Gabriel to Nazareth, a city in Galilee, to a virgin who was engaged to a man named Joseph, a descendant of David's house. The virgin's name was Mary. When the angel came to her, he said, "Rejoice, favored one! The Lord is with you!" She was confused by these words and wondered what kind of greeting this might be. The angel said, "Don't be afraid, Mary. God is honoring you. Look! You will conceive and give birth to a son, and you will name him Jesus. He will be great and he will be called the Son of the Most High. The Lord God will give him the throne of David his father. He will rule over Jacob's house forever, and there will be no end to his kingdom."

Then Mary said to the angel, "How will this happen since I haven't had sexual relations with a man?"

The angel replied, "The Holy Spirit will come over you and the power of the Most High will overshadow you. Therefore, the one who is to be born will be holy. He will be called God's Son. Look, even in her old age, your relative Elizabeth has conceived a son. This woman who was labeled 'unable to conceive' is now six months pregnant. Nothing is impossible for God."

Then Mary said, "I am the Lord's servant. Let it be with me just as you have said." Then the angel left her.

MEDITATION

Joseph and Mary trust that nothing is impossible for God, even in the face of profound unanswered questions. When have you seen or experienced great trust in God even when the future is uncertain? How do you respond to the angel's affirmation that "nothing is impossible for God"?

Day 32

Psalm 80:1-3

Shepherd of Israel, listen!
    You, the one who leads Joseph as if he were a sheep.
    You, who are enthroned
        upon the winged heavenly creatures.
Show yourself before Ephraim, Benjamin,
    and Manasseh!
    Wake up your power!
    Come to save us!
Restore us, God!
    Make your face shine so that we can be saved!

Psalm 23

The LORD is my shepherd.
    I lack nothing.
He lets me rest in grassy meadows;
    he leads me to restful waters;
        he keeps me alive.
He guides me in proper paths
    for the sake of his good name.

Even when I walk through the darkest valley,
   I fear no danger because you are with me.
Your rod and your staff—they protect me.

You set a table for me right in front of my enemies.
You bathe my head in oil;
   my cup is so full it spills over!
Yes, goodness and faithful love will pursue me
   all the days of my life,
   and I will live in the LORD's house as long as I live.

John 10:11-18

"I am the good shepherd. The good shepherd lays down his life for the sheep. When the hired hand sees the wolf coming, he leaves the sheep and runs away. That's because he isn't the shepherd; the sheep aren't really his. So the wolf attacks the sheep and scatters them. He's only a hired hand and the sheep don't matter to him.

"I am the good shepherd. I know my own sheep and they know me, just as the Father knows me and I know the Father. I give up my life for the sheep. I have other sheep that don't belong to this sheep pen. I must lead them too. They will listen to my voice and there will be one flock, with one shepherd.

"This is why the Father loves me: I give up my life so that I can take it up again. No one takes it from me, but I give it up because I want to. I have the right to give it up, and I have the right to take it up again. I received this commandment from my Father."

MEDITATION

*Jesus builds on the metaphor of God as shepherd
to define his relationship with his followers.
The shepherd protects and saves from enemies,
fulfilling a deep human longing. Reflect on
"internal" and "external" enemies in your life.
How are you saved from these enemies?*

DAY 33

Deuteronomy 10:1-5, 10-13

At that time the LORD told me: Carve two stone tablets, just like the first ones, and hike up the mountain to me. Construct a wooden chest as well. I will write on the tablets the words that were on the first tablets—the ones you smashed—then you will place them in the chest.

So I built a chest out of acacia wood and carved two stone tablets just like the first ones. Then I hiked up the mountain holding the two tablets in my hands. God wrote on the new tablets what had been written on the first set: the Ten Commandments that the LORD spoke to you on the mountain, from the very fire itself, on the day we assembled there. Then the LORD gave them to me.

So I came back down the mountain. I put the tablets in the chest that I'd made, and that's where they are now, exactly as the LORD commanded me.

Just as the first time, I remained on the mountain forty days and nights. And the LORD listened to me again in this instance. The LORD wasn't willing to destroy you. Then the LORD told me: Get going. Lead the people so they can enter and take possession of the land that I promised I'd give to their ancestors.

Now in light of all that, Israel, what does the LORD your God ask of you? Only this: to revere the LORD your God by walking in all his ways, by loving him, by serving the LORD your God with all your heart and being, and by keeping the LORD's commandments and his regulations that I'm commanding you right now. It's for your own good!

Ephesians 1:15-23

Since I heard about your faith in the Lord Jesus and your love for all God's people, this is the reason that I don't stop giving thanks to God for you when I remember you in my prayers. I pray that the God of our Lord Jesus Christ, the Father of glory, will give you a spirit of wisdom and revelation that makes God known to you. I pray that the eyes of your heart will have enough light to see what is the hope of God's call, what is the richness of God's glorious inheritance among believers, and what is the overwhelming greatness of God's power that is working among us believers. This power is conferred by the energy of God's powerful strength. God's power was at work in Christ when God raised him from the dead and sat him at God's right side in the heavens, far above every ruler and authority and power and angelic power, any power that might be named not only now but in the future. God put everything under Christ's feet and made him head of everything in the church, which is his body. His body, the church, is the fullness of Christ, who fills everything in every way.

MEDITATION

*God has always asked for devotion and service
from God's people—for Israel to live in God's
commandments and for the body of Christ to
live out our call to be "the fullness of Christ."
In what ways are you living out of the law
of love and serving God with all your being?*

Day 34

2 Samuel 7:1-11, 16

When the king was settled in his palace, and the LORD had given him rest from all his surrounding enemies, the king said to the prophet Nathan, "Look! I'm living in a cedar palace, but God's chest is housed in a tent!"

Nathan said to the king, "Go ahead and do whatever you are thinking, because the LORD is with you."

But that very night the LORD's word came to Nathan: Go to my servant David and tell him: This is what the LORD says: You are not the one to build the temple for me to live in. In fact, I haven't lived in a temple from the day I brought Israel out of Egypt until now. Instead, I have been traveling around in a tent and in a dwelling. Throughout my traveling around with the Israelites, did I ever ask any of Israel's tribal leaders I appointed to shepherd my people: Why haven't you built me a cedar temple?

So then, say this to my servant David: This is what the LORD of heavenly forces says: I took you from the pasture, from following the flock, to be leader over my people Israel. I've been with you wherever you've gone, and I've eliminated all your enemies before you. Now I will make your name great—like the name of the greatest people on earth. I'm going to provide a place for my people Israel, and plant them so that they may live there and no longer be disturbed. Cruel people will no longer trouble them, as they had been earlier, when I appointed leaders over my people Israel. And I will give you rest from all your enemies.

And the LORD declares to you that the LORD will make a dynasty for you. Your dynasty and your kingdom will be secured forever before me. Your throne will be established forever.

Luke 22:14-20

When the time came, Jesus took his place at the table, and the apostles joined him. He said to them, "I have earnestly desired to eat this Passover with you before I suffer. I tell you, I won't eat it until it is fulfilled in God's kingdom." After taking a cup and giving thanks, he said, "Take this and share it among yourselves. I tell you that from now on I won't drink from the fruit of the vine until God's kingdom has come." After taking the bread and giving thanks, he broke it and gave it to them, saying, "This is my body, which is given for you. Do this in remembrance of me." In the same way, he took the cup after the meal and said, "This cup is the new covenant by my blood, which is poured out for you."

Psalm 89:1-4

I will sing of the LORD's loyal love forever.
I will proclaim your faithfulness with my own mouth
from one generation to the next.

That's why I say, "Your loyal love
  is rightly built—forever!
  You establish your faithfulness in heaven."
You said, "I made a covenant with my chosen one;
  I promised my servant David:
  'I will establish your offspring forever;
  I will build up your throne
    from one generation to the next.'"

MEDITATION

*God makes a faithful covenant with David,
and Jesus institutes a new covenant with
his disciples. Both covenants are initiated
out of God's great love for us. Reflect on all
the ways you live in grateful response
to God's loyal covenant love.*

Day 35

Luke 1:46-55

Mary said,
  "With all my heart I glorify the Lord!
    In the depths of who I am I rejoice in God my savior.
  He has looked with favor on the low status
    of his servant.
    Look! From now on, everyone will consider me
      highly favored
      because the mighty one has done great things
        for me.
  Holy is his name.
    He shows mercy to everyone,
      from one generation to the next,
      who honors him as God.
  He has shown strength with his arm.
    He has scattered those with arrogant thoughts
      and proud inclinations.
    He has pulled the powerful down from their thrones
      and lifted up the lowly.
  He has filled the hungry with good things
    and sent the rich away empty-handed.
  He has come to the aid of his servant Israel,
      remembering his mercy,
    just as he promised to our ancestors,
      to Abraham and to Abraham's descendants forever."

1 Samuel 2:1-10

Then Hannah prayed:
My heart rejoices in the LORD.
  My strength rises up in the LORD!
  My mouth mocks my enemies
    because I rejoice in your deliverance.
No one is holy like the LORD—
  no, no one except you!
  There is no rock like our God!

Don't go on and on, talking so proudly,
  spouting arrogance from your mouth,
  because the LORD is the God who knows,
    and he weighs every act.

The bows of mighty warriors are shattered,
  but those who were stumbling
    now dress themselves in power!
Those who were filled full
  now sell themselves for bread,
  but the ones who were starving
    are now fat from food!
The woman who was barren
  has birthed seven children,
    but the mother with many sons has lost them all!
The LORD! He brings death, gives life,
  takes down to the grave, and raises up!
The LORD! He makes poor, gives wealth,
  brings low, but also lifts up high!
God raises the poor from the dust,
  lifts up the needy from the garbage pile.

God sits them with officials,
    gives them the seat of honor!
The pillars of the earth belong to the LORD;
    he set the world on top of them!
God guards the feet of his faithful ones,
        but the wicked die in darkness because no one
            succeeds by strength alone.

The LORD! His enemies are terrified!
    God thunders against them from heaven!
The LORD! He judges the far corners of the earth!

May God give strength to his king
    and raise high the strength of his anointed one.

Psalm 14:1, 7

Fools say in their hearts, There is no God.
    They are corrupt and do evil things;
        not one of them does anything good.

Let Israel's salvation come out of Zion!
    When the LORD changes his people's circumstances
        for the better,
    Jacob will rejoice; Israel will celebrate!

MEDITATION

*In Mary's song of praise we hear an echo
of a prayer from Mary's spiritual ancestor,
Hannah, the mother of the prophet Samuel.
Both women anticipate the reversals of fortune
that will happen when God acts to set the
world right. Reflect on the things that Hannah
and Mary believe will be reversed when
God acts. How does this show God's love?*

DAY 36

Romans 16:25-27

May the glory be to God who can strengthen you with my good news and the message that I preach about Jesus Christ. He can strengthen you with the announcement of the secret that was kept quiet for a long time. Now that secret is revealed through what the prophets wrote. It is made known to the Gentiles in order to lead to their faithful obedience based on the command of the eternal God. May the glory be to God, who alone is wise! May the glory be to him through Jesus Christ forever! Amen.

Ephesians 3:1-6

This is why I, Paul, am a prisoner of Christ for you Gentiles.

You've heard, of course, about the responsibility to distribute God's grace, which God gave to me for you, right? God showed me his secret plan in a revelation, as I mentioned briefly before (when you read this, you'll understand my insight into the secret plan about Christ). Earlier generations didn't know this hidden plan that God has now revealed to his holy apostles and prophets through the Spirit.

This plan is that the Gentiles would be coheirs and parts of the same body, and that they would share with the Jews in the promises of God in Christ Jesus through the gospel.

Colossians 1:10-16, 19-20

We're praying this so that you can live lives that are worthy of the Lord and pleasing to him in every way: by producing fruit in every good work and growing in the knowledge of God; by being strengthened through his glorious might so that you endure everything and have patience; and by giving thanks with joy to the Father. He made it so you could take part in the inheritance, in light granted to God's holy people. He rescued us from the control of darkness and transferred us into the kingdom of the Son he loves. He set us free through the Son and forgave our sins.

The Son is the image of the invisible God,
the one who is first over all creation,

Because all things were created by him:
both in the heavens and on the earth,
the things that are visible
and the things that are invisible.
Whether they are thrones or powers,
or rulers or authorities,
all things were created through him and for him.

Because all the fullness of God
was pleased to live in him,

and he reconciled all things
   to himself through him—
whether things on earth or in the heavens.
   He brought peace through the blood of his cross.

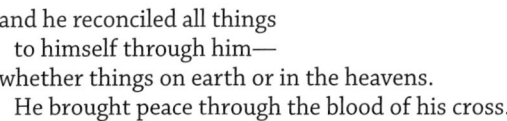

MEDITATION

Paul's benediction to the church at Rome
praises God for the mystery revealed to Paul
and elaborated upon in the other epistles.
God's grace is for everyone, and the saving
work of Jesus Christ is for the whole world.
What individuals or groups of people need to
hear this word about God's love? Are there
people we exclude from this good news?

Day 37

Micah 5:2-5a

As for you, Bethlehem of Ephrathah,
  though you are the least significant of Judah's forces,
    one who is to be a ruler in Israel on my behalf
      will come out from you.
His origin is from remote times, from ancient days.
Therefore, he will give them up
  until the time when she who is in labor gives birth.
  The rest of his kin will return to the people of Israel.
He will stand and shepherd his flock in the strength
  of the Lord,
  in the majesty of the name of the Lord his God.
  They will dwell secure,
  because he will surely become great
    throughout the earth;
  he will become one of peace.

Isaiah 7:10-16

Again the Lord spoke to Ahaz: "Ask a sign from the Lord your God. Make it as deep as the grave or as high as heaven."

But Ahaz said, "I won't ask; I won't test the LORD."

Then Isaiah said, "Listen, house of David! Isn't it enough for you to be tiresome for people that you are also tiresome before my God? Therefore, the Lord will give you a sign. The young woman is pregnant and is about to give birth to a son, and she will name him Immanuel. He will eat butter and honey, and learn to reject evil and choose good. Before the boy learns to reject evil and choose good, the land of the two kings you dread will be abandoned."

Romans 7:21–8:4

So I find that, as a rule, when I want to do what is good, evil is right there with me. I gladly agree with the Law on the inside, but I see a different law at work in my body. It wages a war against the law of my mind and takes me prisoner with the law of sin that is in my body. I'm a miserable human being. Who will deliver me from this dead corpse? Thank God through Jesus Christ our Lord! So then I'm a slave to God's Law in my mind, but I'm a slave to sin's law in my body.

So now there isn't any condemnation for those who are in Christ Jesus. The law of the Spirit of life in Christ Jesus has set you free from the law of sin and death. God has done what was impossible for the Law, since it was weak because of selfishness. God condemned sin in the body by sending his own Son to deal with sin in the same body as humans, who are controlled by sin. He did this so that the righteous requirement of the Law might be fulfilled in us. Now the way we live is based on the Spirit, not based on selfishness.

MEDITATION

Today's passages are about rescue, sometimes from unexpected sources. Reflect on times in your life when you needed to be rescued. When have you seen or experienced rescue from an unexpected source?

DAY 38

Hebrews 10:5-10

Therefore, when he comes into the world he says,
You didn't want a sacrifice or an offering,
but you prepared a body for me;
you weren't pleased with entirely burned offerings
or a sin offering.
So then I said,
"Look, I've come to do your will, God.
This has been written about me in the scroll."
He says above, *You didn't want* and *you weren't pleased*
with a sacrifice or an offering or *with entirely burned offerings*
or a purification offering, which are offered because the Law
requires them. Then he said, *Look, I've come to do your will.*
He puts an end to the first to establish the second. We have
been made holy by God's will through the offering of Jesus
Christ's body once for all.

Romans 3:21-26

But now God's righteousness has been revealed apart
from the Law, which is confirmed by the Law and the Prophets. God's righteousness comes through the faithfulness of

Jesus Christ for all who have faith in him. There's no distinction. All have sinned and fall short of God's glory, but all are treated as righteous freely by his grace because of a ransom that was paid by Christ Jesus. Through his faithfulness, God displayed Jesus as the place of sacrifice where mercy is found by means of his blood. He did this to demonstrate his righteousness in passing over sins that happened before, during the time of God's patient tolerance. He also did this to demonstrate that he is righteous in the present time, and to treat the one who has faith in Jesus as righteous.

Psalm 50:1-15

From the rising of the sun to where it sets,
　　God, the LORD God, speaks, calling out to the earth.
From Zion, perfect in beauty, God shines brightly.
Our God is coming; he won't keep quiet.
A devouring fire is before him;
　　a storm rages all around him.
God calls out to the skies above
　　and to the earth in order to judge his people:
"Bring my faithful to me,
　　those who made a covenant with me by sacrifice."
The skies proclaim his righteousness
　　because God himself is the judge.

"Listen, my people, I will now speak;
　　Israel, I will now testify against you.
　　I am God—your God!

I'm not punishing you for your sacrifices
  or for your entirely burned offerings,
  which are always before me.
I won't accept bulls from your house
  or goats from your corrals
  because every forest animal already belongs to me,
  as do the cattle on a thousand hills.
I know every mountain bird;
  even the insects in the fields are mine.
Even if I were hungry, I wouldn't tell you
  because the whole world and everything in it
  already belong to me.
Do I eat bulls' meat?
  Do I drink goats' blood?
Offer God a sacrifice of thanksgiving!
  Fulfill the promises you made to the Most High!
Cry out to me whenever you are in trouble;
  I will deliver you, then you will honor me."

MEDITATION

*God's love for us finds full expression
in the life, death, and resurrection of Jesus,
and today's readings from Hebrews
and Romans celebrate what Christians
have come to call atonement—"We have been
made holy by God's will through the offering
of Jesus Christ's body once for all."*

How do you understand this great act of love?
With the psalmist, "offer God a sacrifice
of thanksgiving" for Christ's
great sacrifice of love.

Day 39

Luke 1:39-45

Mary got up and hurried to a city in the Judean highlands. She entered Zechariah's home and greeted Elizabeth. When Elizabeth heard Mary's greeting, the child leaped in her womb, and Elizabeth was filled with the Holy Spirit. With a loud voice she blurted out, "God has blessed you above all women, and he has blessed the child you carry. Why do I have this honor, that the mother of my Lord should come to me? As soon as I heard your greeting, the baby in my womb jumped for joy. Happy is she who believed that the Lord would fulfill the promises he made to her."

Luke 14:7-15

When Jesus noticed how the guests sought out the best seats at the table, he told them a parable. "When someone invites you to a wedding celebration, don't take your seat in the place of honor. Someone more highly regarded than you could have been invited by your host. The host who invited both of you will come and say to you, 'Give your seat to this other person.' Embarrassed, you will take your seat in the least important place. Instead, when you receive an invitation, go and sit in the least important place. When your host approaches you, he will say, 'Friend, move up here to a better seat.' Then you will be honored in the presence of all your fellow guests. All who lift themselves up will be brought low, and those who make themselves low will be lifted up."

Then Jesus said to the person who had invited him, "When you host a lunch or dinner, don't invite your friends, your brothers and sisters, your relatives, or rich neighbors. If you do, they will invite you in return and that will be your reward. Instead, when you give a banquet, invite the poor, crippled, lame, and blind. And you will be blessed because they can't repay you. Instead, you will be repaid when the just are resurrected."

When one of the dinner guests heard Jesus' remarks, he said to Jesus, "Happy are those who will feast in God's kingdom."

Matthew 5:1-12

Now when Jesus saw the crowds, he went up a mountain. He sat down and his disciples came to him. He taught them, saying:

"Happy are people who are hopeless, because the kingdom of heaven is theirs.

"Happy are people who grieve, because they will be made glad.

"Happy are people who are humble, because they will inherit the earth.

"Happy are people who are hungry and thirsty for righteousness, because they will be fed until they are full.

"Happy are people who show mercy, because they will receive mercy.

"Happy are people who have pure hearts, because they will see God.

"Happy are people who make peace, because they will be called God's children.

"Happy are people whose lives are harassed because they are righteous, because the kingdom of heaven is theirs.

"Happy are you when people insult you and harass you and speak all kinds of bad and false things about you, all because of me. Be full of joy and be glad, because you have a great reward in heaven. In the same way, people harassed the prophets who came before you."

MEDITATION

What does it mean to be blessed and happy?
These gospel passages open a window on
how we are blessed when we live with humble
dependence on God. Have you ever pondered
Elizabeth's question: "Why do I have
this honor . . . ?" How would you
finish that sentence?

DAY 40

Titus 2:11-14

The grace of God has appeared, bringing salvation to all people. It educates us so that we can live sensible, ethical, and godly lives right now by rejecting ungodly lives and the desires of this world. At the same time we wait for the blessed hope and the glorious appearance of our great God and savior Jesus Christ. He gave himself for us in order to rescue us from every kind of lawless behavior, and cleanse a special people for himself who are eager to do good actions.

Hebrews 1:1-4

In the past, God spoke through the prophets to our ancestors in many times and many ways. In these final days, though, he spoke to us through a Son. God made his Son the heir of everything and created the world through him. The Son is the light of God's glory and the imprint of God's being. He maintains everything with his powerful message. After he carried out the cleansing of people from their sins, he sat down at the right side of the highest majesty. And the Son became so much greater than the other messengers, such as angels, that he received a more important title than theirs.

John 15:7-9

"If you remain in me and my words remain in you, ask for whatever you want and it will be done for you. My Father is glorified when you produce much fruit and in this way prove that you are my disciples.

"As the Father loved me, I too have loved you. Remain in my love."

Philippians 2:1-11

Therefore, if there is any encouragement in Christ, any comfort in love, any sharing in the Spirit, any sympathy, complete my joy by thinking the same way, having the same love, being united, and agreeing with each other. Don't do anything for selfish purposes, but with humility think of others as better than yourselves. Instead of each person watching out for their own good, watch out for what is better for others. Adopt the attitude that was in Christ Jesus:

Though he was in the form of God,
  he did not consider being equal with God
    something to exploit.
But he emptied himself
  by taking the form of a slave
  and by becoming like human beings.
When he found himself in the form of a human,
  he humbled himself by becoming obedient
    to the point of death,
  even death on a cross.
Therefore, God highly honored him

and gave him a name above all names,
so that at the name of Jesus everyone
in heaven, on earth, and under the earth might bow
and every tongue confess that
Jesus Christ is Lord, to the glory of God the Father.

MEDITATION

On this last day of celebration, we give thanks
for the love of God—for the incarnation,
for the teachings of Jesus, for God's power
in resurrection, and for the Holy Spirit,
who empowers us to live as disciples
of Jesus Christ. What is your prayer
of celebration today?